I0370124

99 Zulu Proverbs and Sayings

A Collection of Classic Zulu Expressions, Wise Sayings and Advice

Desaray Wilson-Mnyandu
Phiwokuhle Mnyandu, PhD

© Copyright 2023 by Zulunomics, LLC
All rights reserved.

No part of this book may be reproduced in any form, by photocopy, microfilm, xerography, or any other means, or incorporated into any information retrieval system, electronic or mechanical, without the written permission of the copyright owner.

Library of Congress Catalog Card Number: 2021912334
ISBN: 978-1-7365252-6-5

All enquiries should be addressed to:
Zulunomics, LLC
8145 Baltimore Avenue
STE N334
College Park, MD 20740
info@zulunomics.com
www.zulunomics.com
Zulunomics® is a registered trademark of Zulunomics, LLC.

To our mothers: Nomathamsanqa and Annette. Our first teachers of the proverbs which have taught us lessons, made us laugh, and connected us to our cultures.

Acknowledgements

Over the course of three years, we collected these phrases from casual conversations between ourselves and others. We'd like to acknowledge those who, through their colorful language contributed to our growing list of phrases. We must also give thanks to our brother, Lindokuhle Mnyandu, PhD. His knowledge of Zulu history and generosity with his time was a consequential contribution to this project.

Preface

Like many other cultures in the world, Zulu proverbs and expressions are derived from the simple, observable, lived experiences of daily life. This is in keeping with the rich tradition of passing knowledge down orally from one generation to another.

We hope you, our dear reader, will find this book entertaining, informative, and educational. We have formatted this book to give you more than just a list of phrases, but a peek into Zulu culture and access to the Zulu language in a comprehensive way. Anything that may help you understand more, whether it is culture, general assumptions, prejudices, proclivities, and other aspects of the language which are embedded in these proverbs, we have sought to include it in this book.

When an English speaker uses Zulu proverbs and expressions, often, it is the interpretation that they will quote as they speak or write in English. This is understandable because literal translations may sound nonsensical, especially when there is no context or explanation. However, sometimes it is the translation that sounds good and straight-to-the point and has more fidelity to the meaning of the expression. By including the literal translations, we leave it to you the reader to choose how you want to express and use them in English.

You will find several sayings that contain a reference to "it" followed by parenthesis in the direct translation. Each "it" alludes to the Zulu noun class to which it belongs. In isiZulu, 'it' is determined by the word you're referring to. For example, when referring to a red car, one would say ibomvu (it's red). When referring to a red chair, sibomvu (it's red). When referring to a red sofa, ubomvu (it's red). This conjugation is due to the reference words belonging to different noun classes. Therefore 'it' is not as general of a word in isiZulu as it may be in English!

Finally, a disclaimer. These proverbs and sayings are widespread among the Zulu (and sometimes other Nguni) people. Like most languages, there is intra-lingual diversity. People from different locations and classes may understand the same phrase in a completely different way. It is guaranteed that even a fellow Zulu speaker will read some unfamiliar sayings along with some unfamiliar interpretations in this book. So, please take our version of these sayings with a grain of salt and a sense of humor. The diversity of the Zulu language is one of the things that makes it beautiful. If there are any errors in the interpretation or any other aspects of this work, they are entirely ours. We hope they do not reflect badly on the Zulu language and culture. We are grateful for the feedback we continue to receive from our friends and colleagues across the world.

TABLE OF CONTENTS

FAMILY AND PARENTING

1. **Zinquywa zisemaphuphu**
(The birds' wings) are clipped while they are chicks

2. **Ukuvulela indlela eya komalume**
To pave the way to the (maternal) uncle's place

3. **Akukho chwane lemvubu ladliwa zingwenya qede kwacweba iziziba**
No cub of a hippopotamus is ever eaten by crocodiles and then the rivers remain calm

4. **Ukuqinisa isandla**
To stiffen the hand

5. **Ukuzala ukuzelula**
To give birth is to lengthen one's limbs

PATIENCE PERSEVERANCE AND HARD WORK

6. **Induku elukhuni imila esiweni**
The good stick grows on a cliff

7. **Yoze iyikhothe**
It (cow) will one day lick it (calf)

8. **Kushawa edonsayo**
The one (ox) that is pulling is the one that gets hit

9. **Inhlwa ayibanjwa ngekhanda isavela**
The flying ant is not grabbed by the head when it has barely shown itself

10. **Siyoyicela ivuthiwe**
We will ask for it (meat) when it is cooked

11. **Ukupholisa amaseko**
To cool the hearths

12. **Ukungabuzi Elangeni**
To not bother asking at Elangeni

13. **Ukukhala akusizi, kwahlula imbuzi**
Crying doesn't help, it didn't help the goat

14. **Akulahlwa mbeleko ngakufelwa**
Don't throw away the baby blanket with the death of a child

15. **Ayihlabi ngakumisa**
It (Bull) does not stab by standing still

16. **Akuvelwa kanye kanye, kungemadlebe embongoloi**
People don't all appear at once unlike a donkey's ears

PERIL AND DANGER

17. **Iyabhubhudla inkezo** The gourd is bubbling

18. **Kukhona okusina kukujeqeza**
Something keeps dancing and glancing at you

19. **Ukutheza olunenkume**
To cut a piece of firewood with a centipede inside

20. **Ukuhlangana nemamba iphuze umhluzi**
To encounter a mamba that has drunk soup

21. **Uzowukhomba umuzi onotshwala**
To point out the (house) that has brewed beer

22. **Ukuphuma esamagundwane**
 To exit like rats

23. **Ukukhotha imbenge yomile**
To lick a dry saucer

24. **Ukuvala ngehlahla**
To close or block the way by a branch

25. **Ukuzidonsela amanzi ngomsele**
To draw water towards yourself by the drain

26. **Azilime ziye etsheni**
Let them (cattle) plow to the rock

MANNERS AND DISCRETION

27. **Ukubamba umshini**
To hold the machine

28. **Ukufihla induku emqubeni**
Hide a stick in the hay

29. **Into enhle iyanconywa**
A good thing is complimented

30. **Ukungena umuntu ephaketheni**
To enter someone in the pocket

31. **Kusina kudedelwana**
People dance and then give others a chance

32. **Ukuqhuba intwala ngewisa**
To push excrement by the knobkerrie

33. **Ukukhwela ekhanda**
To climb on the head

LIFE

34. **Ligaya ngomunye umhlathi** It is chewing with the other gum

35. **Amathanga ahlanzela abangena mabhodwe**
The pumpkins grow plentiful for those without pots

36. **Okwenza omude nomfishane kuyomenza**
What happens to a tall person, happens to a short person

37. **Ikhiwane elihle ligcwala izimpethu**
The beautiful fig still gets filled with worms

38. **Akwaziwa ukuthi iyozala inkomoni**
No one knows what type (gender) of cow it will birth

39. **Imbali enhle iyabuna** The beautiful flower withers

MISFORTUNE

40. **Isikhuni sibuya nomkhwezeli** The wood on a fire comes back with the fire tender

41. **Ngiyoyixoxela amagwababa echobana** One day I'll tell it to crows as they groom each other

42. **Kwakhala nyonini?** What type of bird sounded here

43. **Ukufa olwembiza** To suffer a clay vessel's death

44. **Umkhonto ugwaza ekhaya** The spear stabs at home

HAPPINESS

45. **Ukuba phakathi komhlane nembeleko** To be between the back and the baby blanket

46. **Ukuhleka ngelomhlathi** To laugh with the molar

47. **Ukufinya ngendololwane** To wipe one's nose by the elbow

LOVE

48. **Ukuba amathe nolimi** To be saliva and tongue

49. **Lapho amanzi ake ama khona ophinde ame** Where water once stood, it will stand again

50. **Intombi iqoma lapho ithando khona** The girl chooses love wherever she desires

51. **Ukukhotha izithebe** To lick the cutting blocks

LAZINESS

52. **Imbila yaswela umsila ngokulayezela** The hyrax became tailless because it sent others for its own tail

53. **Ukuba umathandukwenzelwa** He/She who likes being done for

54. **Ukuba ukhangezile** To be he/she with hands out

CAUTION AND TAKING CARE

55. **Hamba juba bokuchutha phambili** Fly away dove; they will pluck you ahead

56. **Isalakutshelwa sibona ngomopho** He/She who refuses to learn by being told will learn by events

57. **Lala lulaza ngizokwengula** Sleep, sour milk, so I can take the cream at the top

58. Okungapheli kuyahlola
What does not end is an aberration

59. Ayikho impunga yehlathi
There's no old man in a forest

60. Itshe limi ngothi
The stone is standing on a stick

61. Ukuzwa amanzi ngobhoko
To feel the water by the stick

OPPORTUNITY

62. Ukusina Uzibethele
To seize or take an opportunity quickly

63. Ucilo uzishaya endukwimi
The lark hits itself on the stick

ILLNESS AND DEATH

64. Elokufa alitsheli
The day of death does not announce itself

65. Ukubona ngokusa
To see by morning

66. Kwembulwa kwembeswa They uncover and cover

67. Ukucosha amaphepha kungacelwanga
To pick up trash when no one asked

68. Ukubangwa nezibi
To be fought over/contested with trash

69. Alwehlanga lungehlanga
It has not taken place which has not taken place before

70. Ukuzulelwa amanqe
To be hovered over by vultures

HUMAN RELATIONS

71. Ukuba netiye
To have tea

72. Akukho soka lingena sici There is no ladies' man without a flaw

73. Ukubuza uphale ulimi
To ask and scrape the tongue

74. Isisu somhambi singangenso yenyoni
A traveler's stomach is like a bird's stomach

75. Okoniwe ngomlomo kulungiswa ngomlomo
What gets messed up by mouth gets fixed by mouth

76. Ukuzidlisa satshanyana Eating around (at a place) as if there is grass

77. Ukuqhuqha umuntu upende
To scrape the paint off (of someone)

78. Ukubuza ipasi nesipesheli
Asking for a 'pass' and 'special'

79. **Ichaba ithanbo ijwayele**
It (a dog) chews the bone and gets used to it

80. **Usifumbu ubona uqhaqhazola**
The hunchback points at the shiverer

81. **Umenzi uyakhohlwa kodwa umenziwa akakhohlwa**
The doer forgets but the do-ee never forgets

82. **Sobohla Manyosi!**
It will go down, Manyosi!

83. **Kusuka ijuba kuhlala ungcede**
The pigeon leaves and then the sparrow lands

84. **Ukumila izimpiko**
To grow wings

85. **Induka enhle igawalwa ezizweni**
The good stick is cut from distant lands

86. **Yazwela elimele**
The one that is hurt moos first

DISCRETION

87. **Ukudonsa umuntu ngedlebe**
To pull (a person) by the ear

88. **Indlebe iyaphinga**
The ear is promiscuous

89. **Ithi ingaba nkulu ingazekeki**
Once a story becomes big, it is hard to recount

90. **Ukukhahlelwa ihhashi esifubeni**
To get kicked by a horse on the chest

91. **Ukukubeka kucace okwezinqe zesele**
To make it as clear as a frog's buttocks

92. **Ukudlana indlebe**
To eat each other's ear

93. **Ukukhuluma uze wome amathe**
To talk until saliva dries

94. **Ukugeqa amagula**
To tip the gourds

95. **Ukuchathazela**
To pour a little bit for someone

96. **Ukukhala kwesisicathulo**
The stomping of the shoe

GROWING UP

97. **Ubudoda abukhulelwa**
Manhood need not be grown up to

98. **Umthente uhlaba usamila**
A plant/tree is sharper when it has just come out of the ground

99. **Akukho sihlala saguga namagxolo aso**
There is no tree that gets old with it's (fruits/leaves)

How to use this book

1

Zulu Saying

Literal English Translation

English Interpretation

English explanation and examples of use.

Equivalent or Similar American English Saying

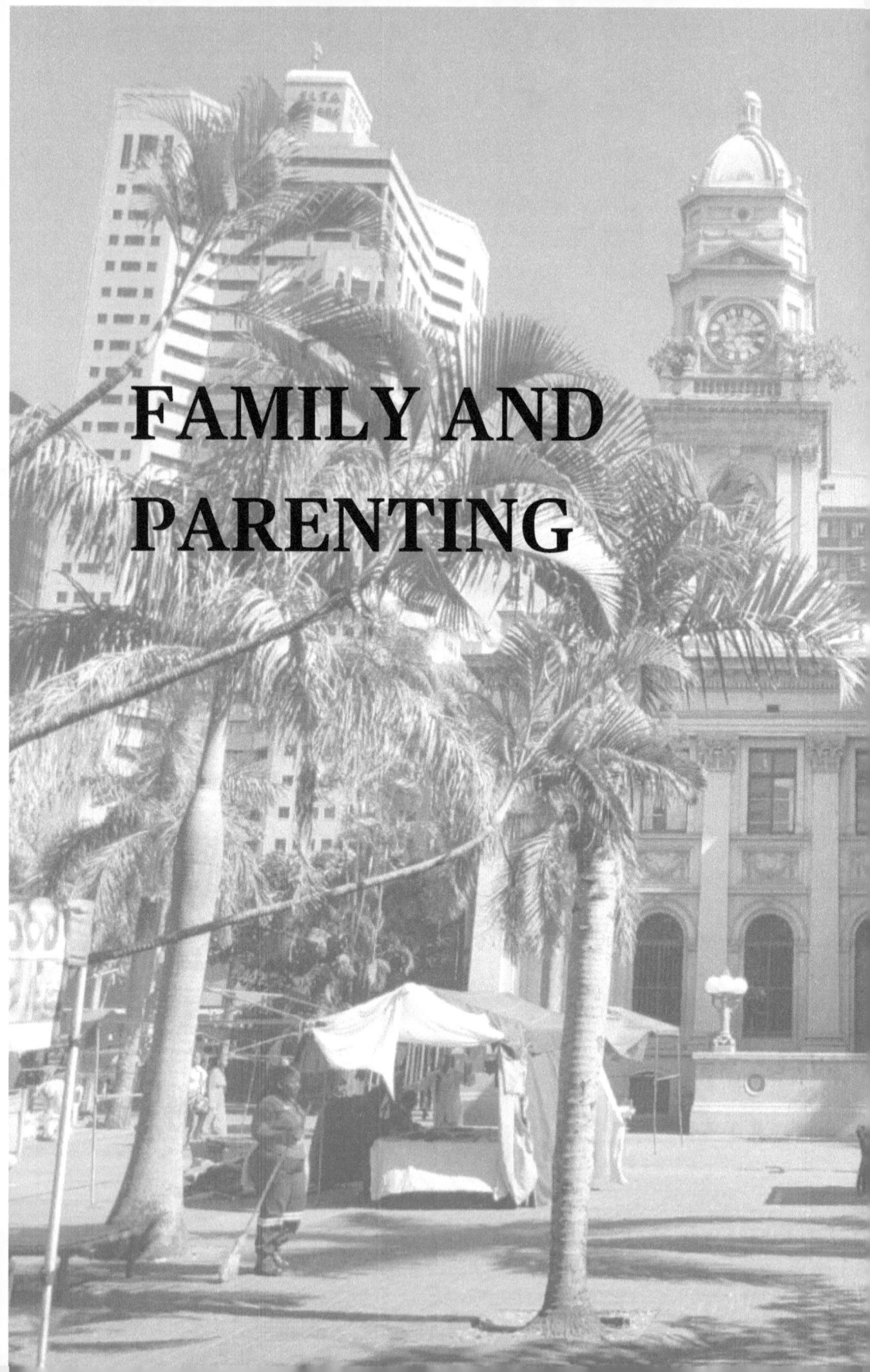

FAMILY AND PARENTING

1

Zinquywa zisemaphuphu

(The birds' wings) are clipped while they are chicks

The best discipline is administered when a child is young

Respect for the family and society is the single most emphasized trait in human relations among Zulu people. As such, the earlier a parent begins to reward good deeds and helps to rid their child of harmful tendencies through good discipline, the better for the child and society. When a parent is reticent to discipline their child, a caring friend or relative may advise 'zinqunywa zisemaphuphu' ('they [birds] are clipped while they are chicks'). Meaning that, like birds whose wings you must clip early if you want to domesticate them, you must discipline children while they are young if you want to make it easier for them to integrate into society.

Spare the rod, spoil the child

2

Ukuvulela indlela eya komalume

To pave the way to the (maternal) uncle's place

To give one a head start

When an adult gives a child a treat, it is common practice for the adult to enjoy a small amount first. For example, before a mom gives her child an apple, they or another present adult will take a little bite out of the apple first. Indeed, the older the adult, the better, for it is considered a blessing. Before they do this, they will often say "Yithi 'ngikuvulele indlela eya komalume" ("Let me open up the way for you to your uncle's home.") To understand this saying fully, you must also know that umalume is a maternal uncle. The most affectionate and pampered relationship is often supposed to be that with your mother's brothers.
So, an adult having a taste of a child's treat is compared to 'opening the way' and is used here as introducing you to something as delightful as a stay at your mother's brother's place.

To take the first crack

3

Akukho chwane lemvubu ladliwa zingwenya qede kwacweba iziziba

No cub of a hippopotamus is ever eaten by crocodiles and then the rivers remain calm

Never mess with the wrong person's child

Hippos and crocodiles live amongst each other with relative tolerance. From time to time, however, crocodiles have been known to try their luck with making a hippo calf their meal, thinking it's an easy catch. They soon find out this is a terrible mistake, as hippos retaliate with excessive aggression. Similarly, some people or things may seem easy to take advantage of but are actually not because their well-being is secured by a much more powerful and able person. Some people are just not to be messed with.

To mess with the wrong person brings no good

4

Ukuqinisa isandla

To stiffen the hand

To put elbow grease

This expression can be used in a range of situations when the added application of effort takes place or a person is diligent towards enforcing a standard of behavior or rules. In a work environment, stiffening the hand can mean you are doing more of a certain physical task (pulling, squeezing, pushing or whatever). In parenting, it can mean being a strict disciplinarian. The same applies to a teacher and their class in school or a manager and their subordinates in a professional setting. So, when someone is working super-hard at a task or is a stickler for applying rules, Zulu speakers will say they are 'ukuqinisa isandla' ('stiffening the hand').

To put elbow grease

5

Ukuzala ukuzelula

To give birth is to lengthen one's limbs

To have children is to stretch yourself

Like many African cultures, having children is expected of Zulu people and considered a duty to one's lineage. According to this perspective, children provide companionship, and as they grow, they are able to do more than you are able to do yourself. In other words, the expectation of a good parent is that they will equip their child to do better and go farther in life. They will be quicker, sharper, more dynamic, achieve more, etc., in ways the parent could not be. The child's achievement, therefore, can always be attributed to the goodness and quality of the parenting. It is as if to say when you become a parent, you gain extra limbs, extra capacity, through your children. If the parents did not finish college, the child will; if they did not have a car, the child will; if they could not live in safety, the child will help them do so, among other things. So, in moments of great achievements, the parents, beaming with pride, will often say, "ukuzala ukuzelula." To give birth is to stretch oneself.

Children are a poor man's riches

PATIENCE
PERSEVERANCE
AND
HARD WORK

6

Induku elukhuni imila esiweni

The good stick grows on a cliff

The best stick is found at great risk

The plants and trees that grow on cliffs are usually stronger and rarer. Successfully getting one of these sticks requires perseverance. Why would you want a rare stick? A person's chosen walking stick has great cultural significance. Traditionally, a person's stick can be used to vote, as identification, to make an oath, and for protection.
With such important uses for a stick, it was important to find one of great quality. Sure, there are sufficient options closer to home. However, only the person who was willing to leave the comforts of home, endure the climb up the cliffs and persevere through the journey back down was able to use the rarest and strongest wood for their stick.

No pain, no gain
Ignore the low-hanging fruit

7
Yoze iyikhothe

It (cow) will one day lick it (calf)

No matter how long the time, what's yours is yours/Your time is coming

When a calf is first born, the mother licks and grooms it, but sometimes it takes a cow a little longer to begin grooming her calf. The grooming is inevitable, although the timing may vary. This saying can be used as encouragement, indicating that a person should be patient because something good is definitely coming.

Every dog has his day
Rome wasn't built in a day

8

Kushawa edonsayo

The one (ox) that is pulling is the one that gets hit

The most ambitious and hard-working person is the one that is most criticized

Within a team of oxen, it is the strongest one that receives the most direction and correction because that is the one that pulls and guides the others. This may not be the one in front. Likewise, it is often the most ambitious, resilient and hard-working person that is most criticized and exposed. Presidents, for example, are held to a higher standard than most because they lead and are supposed to be an example to many others.

The tallest pine gets the most wind
The nail that sticks out gets hammered

9

Inhlwa ayibanjwa ngekhanda isavela

The flying ant is not grabbed by the head when it has barely shown itself

Patience is a rewarding virtue

Historically, and even today, in some places, children collect flying ants to enjoy as a delicacy. It takes a lot of patience to collect many ants because the children must wait for the flying ants to emerge from the hole and then catch them before they fly away. For an impatient child, it would be tempting to try to pluck the flying ant as soon as it is seen, even before it is completely out of its hole. But doing so just breaks the poor insect in half! Sometimes, it is tempting to act recklessly, especially when you are close to reaching your goals. However, it is he who has patience and good timing that is victorious.

Don't jump the gun

10

Siyoyicela ivuthiwe

We will ask for it when it (meat) is cooked

We'll wait and see

Waiting to eat delicious food is hard for everyone. Some people are impatient and constantly pester the cook about having a taste or taking the meat out of the fire early. Others are more patient and wait to eat the meat only when it is fully cooked ('vuthiwe'). When a situation is not so good at a particular moment and Zulu people want to let it play out, they will use this expression. It means they are resigned to how unfavorable things are at that moment, they will reserve judgment for now and will re-visit the issue later. For example, a parent who watches their child continue to engage in dangerous behavior after receiving much advice, tired of it all, will say 'siyoyicela ivuthiwe' ('we will ask for it [meat] when it is cooked'). This is to mean they will no longer engage with the issue and will wait until it comes to a finality.

The proof is in the pudding

11

Ukungapholisa amaseko

To cool the hearths

To not hesitate

Amaseko are the stones used as a hearth in a traditional Zulu kitchen. After cooking is done, the amaseko are hot. It is easy to understand why someone may want to cool them so they can use the area around the cooking place for something else or even to make it safe for a child. But to cool (ukupholisa) the hearth stones takes a while and amounts to a real waste of time for the person doing it. Whenever someone delays something unnecessarily or dilly-dallies, Zulu people call this 'ukupholisa amaseko' ('cooling the hearth stones').

To get down to brass tacks
To get down to business
To not hold one's horses

12

Ukungabuzi Elangeni

To not bother asking at Elangeni

To not hesitate

This common expression comes straight from the life history of the founder of the Zulu nation, the single most revered figure in all Zulu history, King Shaka. Shaka was born out of wedlock since his father, King Senzangakhona, did not want to claim him. His mother, Queen Nandi, fearing for the life of baby Shaka and his brother, Sigujana, left the royal court to raise her children back at her home. Nandi's home was called Elangeni (the place of the sun). As time passed, people back at the royal court began asking about Shaka's whereabouts. When this happened, King Senzangakhona would reply coyly, "Buzani Elangeni" ("Ask in Elangeni"). However, the king was only trying to stall the inevitable talk of his future successor. Since then, this expression ("not asking in Elangeni") has become synonymous with doing something without hesitation.

To get right to it

13

Ukukhala akusizi, kwahlula imbuzi

Crying doesn't help; it didn't help the goat

Whining never helped anybody

Goats are a major source of protein for the Zulu people. So, it is well known that of all the animals, the goat's bleating during slaughter is known to be the loudest. However, no matter how loudly the goat bleats, its fate does not change.
(This expression is not to be misunderstood as meaning that people enjoy the screaming of the goat, whose slaughter is quick and causes minimal pain. It merely uses the goat as a simple analogy to help people understand the point being made.)
Zulu speakers use this phrase when faced with an inevitable and unpleasant situation to discourage complaining. So, when someone asks how they are doing, they may sarcastically reply, "Ngiyaphila. 'Ukukhala akusizi, kwahlula imbuzi." (I am fine. Crying doesn't help, it did not help the goat.)

Crying never helps

14

Akulahlwa mbeleko ngakufelwa

Don't throw away the baby blanket with the death of a child

Never give up

Imbeleko, or 'baby blanket,' is a major part of motherhood in Zulu culture. Like many mothers in Africa, Zulu women wear their children on their backs in order to bond, put the baby to sleep, or free their hands while the baby is awake. A mother will often use the same imbeleko for all her children. If a mother loses a baby, she does not throw away the imbeleko, knowing she might want another baby.
This expression is meant to encourage a person to pick themselves up after a devastating experience, one as tragic as a mother losing her baby. The same way she would not throw away her imbeleko upon the death of her child is the same way a person should not give up on living and enjoying their life, even after a bitter experience.

Where one door shuts, another opens

15

Ayihlabi ngakumisa

It (cow) does not stab by standing still

Stay on the move

Yes, another Zulu expression that uses cows! If you cannot tell already, cows are a major part of Zulu culture. The verb 'misa' ('cause to stop or stand') is key here. Zulu people likely observed that when cows fight, the one that wins is usually the one that moves around. Similarly, in life, a person must not be idle if they want to achieve their goals. They must always be on the move to adapt themselves to changing situations or in order to overcome obstacles.

Without labor, nothing prospers

16

Akuvelwa kanye kanye, kungemadlebe embongolo

People don't all appear at once unlike a donkey's ears

People don't bloom all at the same time

A donkey's ears, most often, stand at the same time, at the same height. However, unlike a donkey's ears, people do not always succeed at the same time or in the same capacities. When a person is being impatient with their own efforts, at the sight of others who seem to be 'making it,' Zulu speakers may tell them "Kuzolunga. 'Akuvelwa kanye kanye, kungemadlebe embongolo.'" ("It will be okay. 'We don't all appear at once like donkey's ears.'")

They also serve those who only stand and wait

PERIL AND DANGER

17

Iyabhubhudla inkezo

The gourd is bubbling

War is coming

War is not a time for foolish haste. Instead, it is a time for careful planning, strategic decisions and (at times) patience. When it was time to go to war, a potion was used to make the men strong, brave and tenacious warriors. Intelezi is a watery herbal mixture. It is kept in a gourd and closed with a top. It is ready when it begins to bubble. It is sprayed on the men's bodies (linkezwa). It is said that whenever a battle is about to begin, even before the men are sprayed, the potion itself begins to bubble (bhubhudla), causing the top of the gourd to move. That bubbling is a sign of impending trouble. This tells the administers, IT IS TIME. Zulu speakers use this saying when referring to an impending conflict or confrontation, especially one in which they feel they have the upper hand. It is hardly ever used with trepidation.

Something is brewing

18

Kukhona okusina kukujeqeza

Something keeps dancing and glancing at you

Something's gonna get you

Imagine you are attending a traditional Zulu dancing (ukusina). The people are gathered in a circle or line. Since it is a public event in a public place, everyone is there - friends and enemies. How does an enemy reveal themselves? According to this expression, they would be dancing in the middle of the crowd but also keeping an eye on you by glancing every few seconds. That is a hallmark of someone of whom you should be suspicious. The Zulu people used this common scene to construct an expression of warning against grave danger, to say 'watch out' or 'I have my eyes on you.' This is given as a last warning to someone that has not listened to prior, more polite warnings. It warns of imminent, negative consequences as a result of that person's actions. Parents may use this expression to bring a child in line when he/she thinks they are getting away with something naughty. When a mother or father, wants to let their child know they are on to them and threaten imminent punishment if they don't stop, they will wag their finger and say 'bhasobha, kukhona okusina kukujeqeza' ('be careful, something keeps dancing and glancing at you').

Dark clouds on the horizon
You'd better watch it

19

Ukutheza olunenkume

To cut a piece of firewood with a centipede inside

To get more than you bargained for

In the days when Zulu people relied on firewood for fuel, women would go out to find it. If a woman found a large piece of wood, she would have to chop (theza) it into smaller pieces in order to bind it into a bunch that could be carried home. Sometimes, in the process of chopping the wood, the woman would get unlucky and chop a piece with a centipede (inkume) inside! The centipede is said to always come out angry and anyone in such a position was said to be in for it!
When a person's actions bring about ferocious and unpleasant outcomes, Zulu speakers will often call this 'ukutheza olunenkume' ('chopping the firewood with the centipede').

To get a nasty surprise

20

Ukuhlangana nemamba iphuze umhluzi

To encounter a mamba that has drunk soup

To get more than you bargained for

South Africa is home to some of the world's most dangerous snakes - the puff adder, spitting cobra, green mamba, and black mamba, among others. So, it is not surprising that snakes are found in many Zulu expressions. While each of these snakes is dangerous, it is the black mamba that is famous for its aggressive behavior. It can be so fierce, in fact, that Zulu people say that it must have drunk (umhluzi) a broth. The broth this saying is referring to is that which contains special herbs and is given to Zulu soldiers to make them strong, brave and tenacious warriors.
Such a mamba would be extraordinarily aggressive and exponentially more dangerous than any other snake to anyone unfortunate enough to cross its path. This is one of a plethora of *threat expressions* (ukusabisa) found in the Zulu language, where the speaker threatens imminent and negative consequences to someone, insinuating if the person crosses the 'red line,' they will really get it, or more ominously, 'uzohlangana nemamba iphuze umhluzi' ('he/she will meet a mamba that has drunk broth')

To get a nasty surprise

21

Uzowukhomba umuzi onotshwala

To point out the (house) that has brewed beer

You will get a bad consequence for your actions

This is expression is straight out of prohibition-like times in South Africa's history, where the apartheid government restricted black South Africans from selling alcohol. Not to be deterred, the people continued brewing their own beer discreetly. When apartheid police would make raids looking for 'moonshine,' instead of going around every house, they would simply catch the first person that looked as if they had been drinking. The person would be subjected to such a terrible beating that it would not take long for them to point out the house with the beer. To this very day, this expression, steeped in the brutality of apartheid, remains a popular *threat expression*. When someone is about to do something bad, like scratch someone's car, for example, and a Zulu speaker wants to convince them of the grave consequences if they do so, they might tell them "uma ukwebha imoto yami, 'uzowukhomba umuzi onotshwala' (if you scratch my car, 'you will point out the house with the beer')."

To get blowback

22

Ukuphuma esamagundwane

To exit like rats

To take off or decamp

Picture a controversial politician at a rally. He's being booed and heckled by a hostile crowd. Imagine the hostility does not stop after the politician has finished his speech. The people just want the politician out of there! The politician must quickly leave the venue to avoid trouble and potential harm. That is 'ukuphuma esamagundwane' ('to exit like rats'). This expression is used to convey a hasty departure or exit from a place, often against your will. It is the retreat made when you want to save yourself from harm or embarrassment, like a rat in a house when a person appears. You do not want to do it, but you *must* do it and do it fast!

To flee
To get (the heck) out of Dodge

23

Ukukhotha imbenge yomile

To lick a dry saucer

To get an unpleasant surprise

Imbenge is an important item in a traditional Zulu kitchen. It is made of weaved grass and shaped like a plate. It has multiple uses. Sometimes it is used to cover the top of a beer container (ukhamba). Sometimes it's used as a small saucer on which to eat snacks like corn or peanuts.
When adults are done eating, children are usually the ones to take the dishes away. They look forward to 'finishing' off whatever the adult has left uneaten on the saucer. A caring adult knows this and never eats everything on a saucer. A few bites of food or even a little sauce to lick from the plate can be a delicious "payment" to a dutiful child. But sometimes an uncaring or greedy adult leaves nothing for the children and even goes so far as to lick the imbenge themselves! So, when a dutiful child comes to take the saucer away and they lick it on the way to the kitchen, with great disappointment, they find out that the saucer is dry! In life, whenever someone experiences sudden and negative consequences or gets a nasty surprise, they are said to 'lick a dry saucer' ('ukhotha imbenge yomile').

To get blowback

24

Ukuvala ngehlahla

To close or block the way by a branch

Massacre or death of an entire family

When a home or building is uninhabitable and too dangerous for anyone to enter, the structure is marked as condemned and boarded up. This expression embodies a very similar situation. Rumored Zulu history says that in the days of widespread sickness, it was decided that chosen leaders should visit each home and determine the health status of all the members. If anyone in a home was found to be infected, the home was to be closed and marked by a large branch. This prevented others from entering through the gate or the door and risking contamination! While stopping the spread of a highly contagious infection, this method of containment also consequently condemned all those inside the blocked homes! This expression is used when Zulu speakers are talking about a devastating event where loss of life took place - a car accident or plane crash where all perish; a family massacre, or a mass shooting, among other sad events where the indiscriminate loss of life takes place.

To annihilate

25

Ukuzidonsela amanzi ngomsele

To draw water towards yourself by the drain

To invite trouble

It rains a lot in Kwazulu-Natal, the traditional 'home' province of the Zulu people. Having a plan for the water run-off that often results from the rain is very important for a typical home. Building a drain, traditionally, is a good way to make sure that a home is not flooded. Of course, the drain is built to direct the water away from or past the home and *not* toward the home. Doing the latter would mean the family would flood its own home.
When a person does something counter-productive or makes a bone-headed mistake that harms their own interests, Zulu speakers will say 'uzidonsela amanzi ngomsele' ('he/she is directing water towards themselves by the drain'). In life, trouble finds you no matter what; there is no need to bring it upon yourself through your own efforts.

To kick a hornet's nest

26

Azilime ziye etsheni

Let them (cattle) plow to the rock

Whatever happens, happens

When a farmer is plowing the land, he takes great care to ensure the cows do not run into big obstacles as they work. A large stone could not only injure the cows but also damage the plow itself! As a precaution, the wisest farmers walk through the field to remove debris before the cows begin plowing. But not all obstacles, like a big rock in the middle of the field, can be moved. The farmer will simply have to direct the cattle to avoid it. However, there may be times the errant cattle just keep pulling towards danger against all the farmer's efforts. At some point, the farmer may give up and think to himself, "So be it."
Similarly, when Zulu speakers are resigned to an imminent and unpleasant fate and willing to take the consequences as they come, they will say 'azilime ziye etsheni' ('let them (cattle) plow to the rock.')

Screw it
What will be, will be

MANNERS AND DISCRETION

27

Ukubamba umshini

To hold the machine

Tolerate mistreatment or subordination

Imagine an old machine that begins to malfunction. It sputters, shudders, shakes and jerks, making it very difficult for the operator to complete his tasks. Instead of stopping to fix the machine, a manager simply tasks the laborer with holding the machine steady until the job is finished. Holding the malfunctioning machine is hazardous and requires long-suffering, tolerance and strength.
A person who tolerates mistreatment or being minimized, who 'takes it' when people mistreat them instead of stopping the bad behavior, is said to 'hold the machine.' On the other hand, if a person does not 'take it' from anyone, people say 'he/she does not hold the machine' ('akawubambi umshini').

To take it

28

Ukufihla induku emqubeni

Hide a stick in the hay

To keep people guessing

To fully appreciate this proverb you have to keep in mind the importance of the stick in Zulu culture, at least in the traditional sense. Among its various uses, a stick was used for fighting. Knowing that a duel is coming up by the hay (where duels often took place), a sneaky boy would hide a stick beforehand, hoping to retrieve it during a fight if things got really nasty and his hands were not enough to win a fight. When a person hides their intentions about something, especially something of keen interest to everybody, waiting to give everybody a surprise, Zulu speakers liken it to hiding a stick in the hay. The person keeps something secret that will give them an advantage later.

To play your cards close to your chest

29

Into enhle iyanconywa

A good thing is complimented

When something is good, it's good

It is human nature to notice and point out problems and bad behaviors. So people should be mindful to give praise and compliments when they are warranted.
In traditional Zulu culture, there is an emphasis on respect and balance in all things, including how one appraises people. This saying is used to avoid sweeping a person's or group's accomplishments and good deeds away with their mistakes.

Give credit where credit is due

30

Ukungena umuntu ephaketheni

To enter someone in the pocket

To undermine someone

Zulu people are both friendly and hospitable. At the same time, though, they are mindful of maintaining their relationships with respectful boundaries.
At work, with friends and even with certain family members, becoming overly familiar can lead to an undermining of position, authority and some basic expectations of respect. In a culture where respect is highly valued, each person should always know their role.
For example, after going out to dinner with his boss, a man starts to see himself as his boss's equal in and out of the office. Soon he becomes too casual with questioning his boss's decisions. He is eventually fired for insubordination or as this saying would say, for entering his boss's pocket!
No matter how close relations are, there is a certain healthy detachment Zulu people believe should exist in all human relations, which prevents negative over-familiarity.

To get out of pocket

31
Kusina kudedelwane

We dance and then give way to others

It is good to give others a chance

During Zulu traditional dancing (ukusina), dancers take turns moving to the center or front to showcase their moves. The expectation is that everyone who steps up will be mindful to not to hog the spotlight. Without being asked or tapped on the shoulder, they should step back after their dance to let others have a turn.
This is applied in all areas where people have a chance to showcase themselves, especially in leadership. A good leader knows when to rule and when to step aside without being told. No matter how good a person is at something, they must always be willing to allow others to shine.

See what others have got

32

Ukuqhuba intwala ngewisa

To push a louse by the knobkerrie

Extreme rudeness

Who would go around poking a tiny louse with a stick? Only a crazy person! And only a crazy person would also be blatantly and unimaginably rude without shame or remorse.
It is accepted in Zulu society that "abantu abafani" all human beings are not alike. Some people are rambunctious, sarcastic, or even contrarian. However, there is a level of rudeness that is not acceptable. Rudeness that hinders the progression or functioning of society, such as loudly arguing in public or cussing at your elders, is considered extreme, intolerable, and (as the saying implies) crazy!

33

Ukukhwela ekhanda

To climb on someone's head

Extreme disrespect

In Zulu culture, the head is revered as the most important part of the human body. As such, how people treat it is very important in portraying respect or lack of it. This is illustrated in how Zulu people typically fuss about the details of a simple act like having a haircut. How, who, or where a person cuts their hair, and even what a person does with their hair once cut, are things not taken lightly. Following in this logic, a person is not allowed to touch the head of someone their senior. If they do, it is considered the height of disrespect and insolence. Therefore, when someone is being openly rude to an adult or anyone in a position of higher authority, Zulu speakers will often say 'ukhwela ekhanda' (he/she is climbing on the head') of that person.

To get out of pocket

34

Ligaya ngomunye umhlathi

It is chewing with the other gum

The situation has changed

Chewing on the other side of your mouth or switching food to the other side can be used when a situation has been turned around, flipped, or switched. For example, someone who was poor but is now rich, or someone who was an atheist but is now very religious, is now "chewing with the other gums."

The wheel of life has turned

35

Amathanga ahlanzela abangena mabhodwe

The pumpkins grow plentiful for those without pots

Good things sometimes go to the non-deserving

A lament for the irony of life, this saying reiterates a theme common in almost all cultures; that you cannot have everything. This specifically targets those who have large endowments that they cannot handle. For example, a person whose father owns a theater, is a bad actor or someone who is rich but financially illiterate. This saying can also be used as an equalizer. It can seem that someone who is wealthy, intelligent, or beautiful has everything, but even they don't have it all.

You can't always have it all

36

Okwenza omude nomfishane kuyomenza

What happens to a tall person, happens to a short person

There are some things that happen to everyone

Sometimes, it may seem like bad things only happen to a certain people. It is easy, to think so, especially when you are on the receiving end of misfortune. Not so, according to this proverb. Stuff happens, to everyone, without regard to a person's physical attributes.

It rains on the rich and the poor

37

Ikhiwane elihle ligcwala izimpethu

The most beautiful fig still gets filled with worms

Beauty fades

Figs are a sweet and tasty treat that grow in warm climates, including South Africa. However, one thing that is not so tasty is the worms that are commonly found inside them. And as the saying says, even the most beautiful figs still gets worms.
This saying is most commonly applied to someone's physical appearance, usually a beautiful woman. Even the most gorgeous woman can have "worms" or undesirable qualities.
This saying can also describe tempting situations that look wonderful but have an intolerable caveat.
Whatever the application, it is wise not to make decisions solely based on exterior beauty or first impressions.

Don't judge a book by its cover

38

Akwaziwa ukuthi iyozala inkomoni

No one knows what type (gender) of cow it will birth

We are not sure of the outcome

A calf has a fifty percent chance of being born male or female. Even with such high odds, either way, it is still impossible to know the gender of the calf (without an invasive and unnecessary medical procedure). All interested parties must simply wait for the outcome.
Similarly, when there is no way to determine the outcome of a situation, a Zulu speaker may use this saying to encourage people to stop wasting time with guesses and wait.

Your guess is as good as mine
It's anyone's guess

39

Imbali enhle iyabuna

The beautiful flower withers

Beauty fades

A The beauty of a flower is appreciated universally. The bright colors and sweet smells of flowers are attractive to animals, insects and humans alike. However, for all its splendor, the beauty of a flower is on display for only a short time.
Just as all the flowers, including the most beautiful, eventually wither, the outer beauty of a person eventually fades. This saying can be used to encourage people to seek deeper and more meaningful relationships. It can also be a comfort to people as they grow older because aging is an inevitable part of life for everyone.

All good things must come to an end

MISFORTUNE

40

Isikhuni sibuya nomkhwezeli

The wood on the fire comes back with the fire tender

Something counter-intuitive happens

When a person is tending a fire (ukukhwezela), they will most likely be putting wood into the fire, not removing it. This is what is expected of a fire tender (umkhwezeli). So, it would come as a surprise, then, if umkwezeli began to pull out firewood from the fire. When someone does something unexpected, bringing about a surprising and unpleasant outcome, Zulu people will say 'isikhuni sibuya nomkhwezeli' (the piece of firewood is returning with the fire tender'). In other words, it is something that really should not be happening.

I did not see that coming

41

Ngiyoyixoxela amagwababa echobana

One day I'll tell it to the crows as they groom each other

I'll never forget it

You'll hear this coy phrase being used by a Zulu speaker after a nasty or bewildering experience.
Being betrayed in love or being conned by a trusted partner are just a couple of examples.
Upon finding out the truth, with resigned bitterness, accepting the totality of their dismay, often accompanied by a deep sigh and proverbial double-clapping of the hands, the victim will declare "Angikaze ngikuubone lokhu, ngiyoyixoxela amagwababa echobana" (I have never seen something like this, I will re-tell it to the crows as they groom each other").
As birds which Zulu people are not typically expected to interact with, the fact that a victim will recount their experience to them is meant to symbolize the depth of the bitterness the victim feels, such that they would even tell the ominous crows themselves.

I'll be damned

42

Kwakhala nyonini?

What type of bird sounded here

What the heck happened?

In Zulu culture, different birds are said to represent different signs or carry different energy. If a certain bird visits a Zulu home, Zulu people generally believe it portends the energy associated with that bird.
An African hoopoe (ungomfi) call signals an imminent visit from a welcomed guest or good fortune. However, when a hamerkop (uthekwane) lands on a home, it signifies death or other misfortune.
If something bad or perplexing keeps happening (all your appliances breaking down in the same week or your family continually getting sick) despite attempts to stop it, Zulu speakers, short of all logical explanations, may assume there are other forces at work and will ask in lamentation, 'Kwakhala nyonini?' ('What type of bird sounded?').

43

Ukufa olwembiza

To suffer a clay vessel's death

Something very bad and irreversible, a bad omen

Imbiza is a relatively large-sized vessel in which Zulu people traditionally store food, especially grain. It is made of clay and quite delicate. It is so delicate that children are usually not allowed unsupervised around it. You can only imagine what happens when an imbiza breaks and the family's grain is scattered all over the place, mixed up with small pieces of clay. It is very difficult to recover the grain and nearly impossible to repair the vessel. Not only is the destruction irreversible, but it also compromises the family's food security.

When something bad happens in a person's life, something calamitous and irreversible, including the death of a loved one, Zulu people will compare the irreparable harm of such a loss to the breaking of the food vessel and cry, 'Sife olwembiza' ('We have died the death of the food vessel').

44

Umkhonto ugwaza ekhaya

The spear stabs at home

Tragedy from within

Although sad, it is not out of the ordinary for unfortunate things to happen to a family. However, it is notable if those unfortunate things are brought about by someone within the home. In Zulu culture, a spear is an important tool intended to defend the family from outside danger. It is used in slaughtering cows for food and in other important spiritual ceremonies of the family. The spear is the one thing in a home that represents the family itself - its authority, survival, potency, etc. It is especially tragic and even a bad omen when the family's own spear is used to harm someone within the family. In life, when someone from within a family, group, community, class, office, and so forth does something to harm the very same unit, it is viewed as exceptionally tragic and a bad omen. It is as if a family's spear has been used to harm a family member.

Own goal

45

Ukuba phakathi komhlane nembeleko

To be between the back and the baby blanket

Very comfortable

There are few places on earth a human being feels the most cared for and secure than a baby on their mother's back. Like many women in the world, Zulu mothers still carry their babies on their backs, whether to comfort them when they cry, put them to sleep, or just to bond more. The blanket used to carry the baby on the back, amongst other things, is called 'imbeleko.' This popular expression is applied not just to children. When a person of any age is living a safe and comfortable life or is being well treated in any relationship (in a marriage, by colleagues at work, etc.), Zulu speakers will say 'uphakathi komhlane nembheleko' ('he/she is between the back and the baby blanket').

To have it made

46

Ukuhleka ngelomhlathi

To laugh with the molar

Extreme happiness

Zulu speakers use this expression when describing a person who finds something so hilarious or is so happy that they their mouth is agape and most teeth can be seen as they laugh or smile, especially the molars. This is called 'ukuhleka ngelomhlathi' ('laughing with the molar').

Belly laugh

47

Ukufinya ngendololwane

To wipe one's nose by the elbow

To feast

Imagine you are sitting and enjoying an incredible barbecue. Your hands, mouth, and quite possibly your shirt are covered in a tasty sauce. You are feasting! What would you do if suddenly your nose began to itch? Perhaps you would use your elbow to wipe your nose! Your hands are so occupied with food that you wipe your nose with your elbow. This saying can be used to indicate that someone is literally or figuratively feasting!

48

Ukuba amathe nolimi

To be saliva and tongue

Extremely close

What can be closer than your tongue and saliva? Not much! This is why Zulu people use this imagery to describe people or things that are extremely close. This can be used for friends, colleagues, family and even animals. Zulu people will say "Banga mate nolimi" - they are like saliva and tongue.

Like two peas in a pod

49

Lapho amanzi ake ama khona ophinde ame

Where water once stood, it will stand again

A repeat will happen

The waters of South Africa follow a cycle, but not necessarily a timeline. Streams, lakes and rivers rise, fall, flow and stagnate as seasons change, when droughts come and in times of lots of rain. While one may not exactly know when a river may rise or a stream may stop again, you can be sure that it will happen.
Zulu speakers use this analogy to express nostalgia for a beautiful juncture or time in life. Good things, seasons and events will happen in life and although the timeline is not always clear, it is sure that those good things will happen again.
This saying can be used to get back with an ex-lover, recover a friendship or renew an old acquaintance and signifies an optimism that with the passage of time, there is renewal.

History repeats itself

50

Intombi iqoma lapho ithando khona

The girl chooses love wherever she desires

Freedom

In Zulu culture there is wide latitude for choosing a spouse. There are no arranged marriages, and in general, it is considered fruitless to force someone to love. Likewise, it is futile to dissuade love. The more you try to separate lovers, the more they are drawn together.
This saying can be used as a lament or a celebration. For example, if a woman chooses to marry the town's "bad boy," her parents may be reminded that they should not interfere because their daughter can "choose love wherever she desires." However, that same woman may celebrate her freedom to choose love by quoting this saying during her 20th wedding anniversary!

51

Ukukhotha izithebe

To lick the cutting blocks

Taking the scraps

Eating meat is usually a communal event in Zulu culture. One large piece of meat is placed on a cutting board, cut into pieces, and shared with everyone. If someone is busy or late, they, unfortunately, may have only scraps to eat or the cutting board to lick.
Thus, partaking in something at a lower standard or in something that once belonged to someone else is likened to 'licking the cutting blocks."
Going out with your friend's ex, for example, is a quick way to be labeled as someone who "licks the cutting blocks."

Taking someone's leftovers

52

Imbila yaswela umsila ngokulayezela

The hyrax became tailless because it sent others for its own tail

Not everything should be delegated

A Zulu myth recounts the beginning of the world when the creator summoned all the animals to come and receive their tails. One by one, the animals made their way. As the leopard, the elephant, and the monkey went, the hyrax asked each of them to also bring his tail. They each returned with their own tail but without a tail for the hyrax. Tired of disappointment, the hyrax finally went to the creator himself. When he arrived, the creator said there were no more tails left. The hyrax learned that some things in life are too important to delegate to others.
When someone is lazily delegating tasks that they should do themselves, this saying is a great reminder that the consequences could be very unpleasant.

If you want something done right, you must do it yourself

53

Ukuba umathandukwenzelwa

He/She who likes being done for

Extreme laziness

Zulu culture consistently warns about laziness. It is regarded as a gateway habit to other, more reprehensible, character traits. And so it is that Zulu speakers have quite a few expressions to describe lazy behavior or lazy people, none of which are flattering. Indeed, there is even a categorization of the levels of laziness. The word "umathandukwenzelwa" comes from 'thanda' (like/love), 'ukwenzelwa' (to be made for). Simply put, then, a person who is umathandukwenzelwa is one that likes nice things but does not like to go through the hard work it takes to obtain them. Everything must be done for this type of person. This is a type of behavior scorned in Zulu culture.

To be a couch potato

54

Ukuba ukhangezile

To be he/she with hands out

To be a mooch or beggar

To have your hands open and out is a universal gesture for asking. If someone is constantly asking for things, money, or favors, they may be labeled as a beggar, a mooch, or "one with his/her hands out."

To be a freeloader

CAUTION AND TAKING CARE

55

Hamba juba bokuchutha phambili

Fly away dove, they will pluck you ahead

Go away, but they will get you where you're going

Partly a wish and partly a curse, this expression is used by a person who has been wronged or had their trust betrayed in a serious way. When love, marriage, friendship, partnerships, or any other relationship goes awry, there is a chance that the offender may completely lack remorse.

When it becomes clear to the victim that there is nothing they can do to get even or salvage a modicum of justice, they will use this phrase in the hopes that the offender will later feel how they feel. Many people perceive this expression as *ukusonga*, a fervent oath, threat or prayer of ill will towards someone that has done you wrong. Zulu people take this very seriously. So serious, in fact, that after hearing this, they may seek a session with their pastor, *isangoma*, or both!

Your karma is coming

56

Isalakutshelwa sibona ngomopho

He/She who refuses to learn by being told will learn by events

He/She who will not learn from advice, will learn from experience

It is infinitely better to learn by heeding advice versus learning through experience. The consequences of not listening are usually unpleasant and bitter. However, by putting aside pride and listening to the council of the elderly and experienced, these consequences can be avoided.

57

Lala lulaza ngizokwengula

Sleep, sour milk, so I can take the cream at the top

Silly goose

One of the Zulu people's favorite foods, amasi (sour cream), is still consumed today in South Africa. To harvest amasi, milk is stored and cultured. Over time, the delicious cream rises, and the bitter, watery by-product (umlaza) sinks.
This process was compared to someone taking advantage of the naïveté of another. There is an abundance of characters waiting to take advantage or 'cream the top' of someone who is naïve, after get-rich-quick schemes, or is easily tricked. A victim's lack of self-awareness makes them sink like sour milk, and they get 'creamed' (or scooped like cream) as a result.
It's as if you can practically hear the scammer mischievously say, 'lala lulaza, ngizokwengula' (sink sour milk so I can take the cream at the top).

Buttering someone up

58

Okungapheli kuyahlola

What does not end is an aberration

All good things must come to an end

Umhlola is an aberration or an inexplicable abnormality that is often unsettling and portends bad things, an omen. This comes from the verb 'hlola', meaning to blight with bad luck or energy. So, when people are having such a good time that they do not want an event to end, someone dismissing them may say, "okungapheli kyahlola." This is to mean, yes, we are having a good time, but we all know that anything that does not end is unnatural and, as a result, unsettling and even omen-inducing.

Here today, gone tomorrow

59

Ayikho impunga yehlathi

There's no old man in a forest

The rules of society do not apply in the wilderness

In Zulu culture, as in many African societies, old age means an automatic bestowal of respect as well as deference in many matters. In any discussion, the old person with white hair (impunga) is listened to intently. People rarely contradict him/her publicly, even when they disagree with them. Not so in the bush or in a wild-wild- west-type situation. No regard is given to such things as old age. The rules of propriety, strictly observed in a normal society, are not expected to be respected in a wild setting where survival is the primary motivation for most actions. This may refer to a society where things have devolved to such a primal level, and the first sign of such a decline is the ending of respect for elders.

There is no honor among thieves

60

Itshe limi ngothi

The stone is standing on a stick

The situation is precarious. Things are bad

It was a precarious situation, a trap had been set, and Nkombose was unaware. His sister, an intelligent advisor and lieutenant, intervenes and warns him amid the plotters, using allegories and coded language that only he would understand lest he faces demise. She gives the infamous warning that became part of Zulu folklore. "Nkombose kababa, wake walibonaphi itshe limi ngothi? (Where have you ever seen a stone standing on a stick?)"

In a practical sense, this expression comes from the experience of trapping birds. Of the many traps that can be used, doves are particularly susceptible to deadfall traps in which a heavy stone is balanced on a stick over a bait. Smaller, more nimble birds stand nearby and call out... almost as if to warn the doves saying, "a stone standing on a stick is not natural!" Likewise, this saying is an artful and discreet way to call attention to a trap, a setup, or something that is just off.

61

Ukuzwa amanzi ngobhoko

To feel the water with a stick

Test a situation

Before crossing a river, people test the depths of the water and survey the terrain using a stick. Crossing is a serious task; not testing or fully evaluating the river's depth can lead to death. Likewise, to avoid unexpected difficulty, it is advisable to have a plan, to evaluate, and to acclimatize yourself to a situation before completely jumping in.

To feel/check something out
To test the waters

OPPORTUNITY

62

Ukusina uzibethele

To dance and crucify yourself

To seize or take an opportunity quickly

Ukusina is (traditional Zulu) dancing. 'Ukuzibethela' means 'to drink a lot.' (Interestingly, it comes from the verb 'bethela' ['crucify']). So, when a person gets very drunk, Zulu speakers view them as crucifying or nailing themselves!] This common expression is used for things beyond drinking, however. When a person has a lot of fun at an event, feasts on something, seizes a given opportunity to the max, or does anything enjoyable without reservation, that person is said to be 'dancing and nailing themselves' ('uyasina uyazibethela').

To stuff oneself
To pig out

63

Ucilo uzishaya endukwimi

The lark hits itself on the stick

To be very lucky

Back in the day, when boys were out herding cattle, they would also hunt for birds to roast for lunch. Ucilo is a small bird that is hard to catch or trap. Also, the usual assumption is that when hunting, it is the hunter who hits the prey with their stick. How unusually lucky the boys would be if ever the lark itself actually ran onto the stick! That is exactly what this expression is about. When someone is just minding their business and going about their day and a good opportunity suddenly presents itself, Zulu speakers will say, 'ucilo uzishaya endukwini' ('the lark ran onto the stick'). In other words, they are suddenly at the receiving end of a coincidence with a positive outcome.

Something falls on one's lap
It just fell from the sky

ILLNESS AND DEATH

64

Elokufa alitsheli

The day of death does not announce itself

You never know when your day will come

No matter how happy and fortunate the present moment of our lives may be, it is difficult to predict or foresee the day of death or any misfortune that may befall us. A person never knows when their luck will run out.

To ride high in April and be shot down in May
Life comes at you fast

65

Ukubona ngokusa

To know by each morning

To be day by day

Someone is very sick, and their recovery is so much in doubt that loved ones no longer know whether each dawn that breaks will find that person alive or not. Their life is hanging in the balance and things can go either way. When a person is this sick, Zulu speakers will say "kubonwa ngokusa (we know by each morning)," meaning if the person is alive this morning, the next morning we may well find out they are not.

To have a 50-50 chance to live
To be deathly ill
To be gravely ill

66

Kwembulwa kwembeswa

They uncover and cover

Close to death

A person is extremely sick, bed ridden, and close to death. The person's condition has deteriorated such that there is no guarantee that they will see another day. Zulu people will then use the expression "Kwembulwa kwembeswa" (the blankets are uncovered and they are covered) The person's condition is so bad that throughout the day the family opens the blanket or uncovers to see if they are still alive....then repeats until the person gets better or dies. It can also be said that there's an element of helplessness on the part of the family or caregivers. Having exhausted all options for care, they must now just wait and check and wait and check.

To be deathly ill
To be gravely ill

67

Ukucosha amaphepha kungacelwanga

To pick up trash when no one asked

To go crazy

This expression is used to describe a condition in which a person is mentally unwell in a severe and public way. It was observed that some mentally unwell individuals would resort to vagrant behavior where they would wander around doing what to most people seemed like picking up little pieces of paper and trash there and there. It is then that the expression "ucosha amaphepha kungacelwanga" was derived. It refers to the aimless wandering of a mentally unwell person. This has come to be used to refer to someone exhibiting odd behavior closely resembling a mentally unwell individual.

To not play with a full deck
To be off your rocker

68

Ukubangwa nezibi

To be vied for with trash

To be extremely sick

Religiously, every morning, every Zulu home is swept. Normal debris, food and izibi (dust, dirt and specks) are all removed without hesitation.
If someone's life is in a precarious situation, they are said to be in a position to be swept out like the morning trash. The person is just so physically unwell (not of their own doing) that their life is in danger of being swept from the home.
This saying is a strong analogy used to express the daily worry about losing the sick person and does not equate the sick person's life with trash. Concerned friends and family may say, "We're contesting your life with trash! You're almost dying. Every morning we must rescue you from being "swept out!"

To be critically ill

69

Alwehlanga lungehlanga

Nothing has happened that has not happened before

Condolences

When death strikes, as it often does in human life, Zulu speakers will often seek to comfort the bereaved by telling them "akwehlanga lungehlanga." Meaning, 'however painful the loss may be, be comforted in that it happened to some of us too, and hence as we recovered, so shall you.' It has not befallen you that has not befallen others too. It is said not to be dismissive of the bereaved person's pain or to undermine their loss but to strengthen them with the knowledge that they will survive their loss, just as others have.

Take heart
Hang in there

70

Ukuzulelwa amanqe

To be hovered over by vultures

To be in danger or a precarious situation

Deep in the wilderness a wounded, limping lion is followed by vultures, birds of prey that scavenge on dead animals, looking forward to its death. In the same way, someone who is in grave danger or is facing impending doom is said to 'be hovered over by vultures.'

The 'doomed' situation may not always involve physical harm. It can be about getting fired, having a possession repossessed, or being expelled from school, and Zulus will tell you, "Ukuzulelwa amanqe." In a domestic environment, a strict parent may tell this to a child as a last warning for a grave infraction.

To skate on thin ice
Be in deep water
Be in a pretty pickle
Be up a creek without a paddle

71
Ukuba netiye

To have tea

To practice favoritism

Picture a group of people sitting around a table having tea! They will likely have an intimate discussion on various topics. Suffice it to say, people that have such 'tea' will more often, rather than seldom, be part of a clique or group of insiders. Zulu people use this expression when someone is practicing favoritism. It is when they give preferential treatment to certain 'insiders' or members of their favored clique as if they share tea often. Someone in a work environment, a teacher with certain students, etc. All can be said to 'have tea' if they unfairly favor some people over others in an overt way.

To play favorites

72

Akukho soka lingena sici

There is no ladies' man without a flaw

No one is perfect

An 'isoka' is a ladies' man. It is a person that is popular with girls in a way that is not viewed in a negative light in Zulu culture. He is not just suave but well-mannered and an all-round polished person. However, no matter how many good qualities an isoka may have for all to see, they always have some flaw that a person that observes them long enough will notice. Zulu people use this expression for all people, that no matter how many good attributes a person may have, they will still have a flaw, after all, 'akukho soka lingenasici salo' ('There is no ladies' man without a flaw.'). If an isoka who is loved by many people has flaws, what of the 'regular' folks?

Every rose has its thorn

73

Ukubuza uphale ulimi

To ask and scrape the tongue

Question extensively

This expression is used when someone is asking too many questions about a particular issue without relenting. Every answer you give is followed by another question. It is as if they are 'scraping the words off your tongue as they question, looking for specific answers.

Put through the wringer
Put on the hot seat
Give the third degree

74

Isisu somhambi singangenso yenyoni

A traveler's stomach is like a bird's stomach

A traveler won't eat too much

Zulu people, like many African peoples, have been known for being hospitable to strangers. This expression encourages hospitality, especially the importance of feeding the traveling stranger. They will not eat all your food. Indeed, aware of the sacrifice you have gone through in providing them sustenance, a good traveler will never eat all the food given, which would be taking advantage of the hospitality. It is this cultural practice that gave birth to the expression 'isisu somhambi singangenso yenyoni.' In the old days, the traveler who was overcome by darkness, seeking shelter and sustenance from any nearby home, would often mouth this expression as they announced themselves at the gate.

Living out of a suitcase

75

Okoniwe ngomlomo kulungiswa ngomlomo

What gets messed up by mouth, gets fixed by mouth

Things can always be talked out

Don't involve violence if it can be fixed by talking. If someone offends you with their words, you must use words to resolve it and not violence. That is the simple sentiment of this expression. Zulu speakers use it a lot when they are in the wrong and they want to talk things out with the person they offended - which often works! Mature and well-meaning adults are able to overcome things through discussion.

To bury the hatchet
To cut the gordian knot

76

Ukuzidlisa satshanyana

Eating around (at a place) as if there is grass

To hang around a place/person

Yep, yet another Zulu expression involving cows. Surprise, surprise! When cattle are grazing, there is inevitably a fight or sparring. Later, when a cow wants to 'reconcile' with another, it will pretend as if it is interested in the grass around the area where the other cow is eating. It is as if there is no grass anywhere else except in this one spot. The cow is not interested in the grass there; it simply wants to be next to the other cow. It is angling.
When someone has offended you, or when they simply want to gain your favor or attention, they will often hang around where you are. In a room full of empty chairs, they will come and sit on the one right next to yours. Zulu people will often say the following about this person: 'uzidlisa satshanyana' ('he/she is eating around [a place] as if there is grass there').

To mill around
To act all friendly

77

Ukuqhuqha umuntu upende

To scrape the paint off (of someone)

To really 'deal' with someone/ frustrate someone

Scraping paint off a wall is difficult. For the job to be complete, it must be done evenly, completely and thoroughly. When a person deals with you, confounds you, or gives you a hard time, and they do it so thoroughly you cannot get them back, Zulu speakers will say 'ukuqhuqhe upende' ('he/she scraped the paint off of you').
For example, if students misbehave so much toward a teacher that the teacher losses all control of the classroom and is completely out of options for dealing with the situation. It is as if the teacher was a wall and the students scraped him clean.

To put someone through the wringer

78

Ukubuza ipasi nesipesheli

Asking for a 'pass' and 'special'

To be nosy

This expression is straight out of the dark days of apartheid, where the movement of black people around South Africa was tightly controlled. If you were black, you needed to have a 'pass' in order to avoid arrest when simply walking in the city. You could have a 'special pass' if you needed to linger after curfew or as your employment situation dictated. The first thing a policeman demanded whenever they stopped a black person was their pass or special.

Long after apartheid rule ended, whenever someone is being pesky by asking all sorts of questions or being nosy, be it a child or a nosy friend, Zulu speakers will say 'ungibuza ipasi nesipesheli' ('he or she is asking me for a "pass" and "special"').

To poke your nose into an issue

79

Ichaba ithambo ijwayele

It (a dog) chews the bone once and gets used to it

Lack of gratitude

Whenever you give a dog a bone, especially if it is a neighbor's dog, one which you are not obligated to feed, it often gets used to getting fed by you at a particular time, at a particular spot. If you give it a bone by the gate, you soon find it waiting for you there, expecting a bone all the time, whether you are ready to feed it or not. This expression is used for ungrateful people who get help once but then expect it all the time and, indeed, feel entitled to it. When Zulu speakers see this, they will often say 'ichaba ithambo ijwayele' ('once it [the dog] chews the bone once it then gets used to it').

Give someone a hand and they take an arm

80

Usifumbu ubona uqhaqhazola

The hunchback points at the shiverer

Being a hypocrite

Usifumbu ('a hunchback') is someone who, according to this expression, would be expected to have a natural sympathy for others with disabilities. But alas, sometimes the hunchback will be found pointing out uqhaqhazela ('a shiverer') and even making fun of them. When a person mocks others or is hypocritical in how they point out others' flaws while they themselves have an obvious one, Zulu speakers will often say, ' usifumbu ubona uqhaqhazela.'

The pot calling the kettle black
Throwing stones while living in a glass house

81

Umenzi uyakhohlwa kodwa umenziwa akakhohlwa

The doer forgets but the recipient of the deed never does

A deed is never forgotten.

Zulu people are often moved by unexpected gestures of kindness. On the other hand, they are also indelibly affected by bad actions or acts of bad faith. Be that as it may, they never forget these deeds if they are the recipients of them (umenziwa). Long after the doer has forgotten, Zulu people will often go out of their way to seek the person out and thank them for a good deed. On the other hand, if a bad deed is done, they will often use this expression to show their satisfaction if the bad person gets what is coming to them.

Forgive but never forget

82

Sobohla, Manyosi

It (the belly) will one day shrink, Manyosi!

One day you'll remember me

Manyosi was a brave and distinguished man. He was favored and trusted by King Shaka, who provided Manyosi with great wealth. During his time of plenty, Manyosi was proud and selfish. He hoarded his wealth so much that he grew a large belly (umkhaba). After King Shaka's death, in the rivalry of the royal factions, Manyosi switched sides.

After switching, Manyosi was warned, "Okwamanje sikhukhumele isisu, kodwa sobohla Manyosi. (For now, your belly is full, but one day it will shrink)." Whatever had been sustaining him after he switched sides would eventually prove to be nothing in the long run.

Manyosi quickly discovered that this foreshadowing was correct, and he had made a terrible mistake. The opposing side was not nearly as generous, and his infamous belly began to shrink.

Similarly, when Zulu people feel betrayed, they compare the betrayer to the legendary Manyosi and declare 'Sobohla (it will one day shrink)."

Karma will find you

83

Kusuka ijuba kuhlala ungcede

The pigeon leaves and then the sparrow lands

To be a bad replacement for someone

The sparrow is a songbird known for its small size. When a person takes over a position or a job that others think he/she cannot measure up to, Zulu people will compare that to a sparrow replacing a pigeon. While colorful and active, the sparrow is still considerably small when compared to a pigeon. This same imagery is used to discuss a situation in which a new person is perceived as falling short in their responsibilities in contrast to their predecessor. It is as if a pigeon has flown off from its perch and has not been replaced by an equal.

To have big shoes to fill
To not be able to hold a candle next to someone

84

Ukumila izimpiko

To grow wings

To think you're all that

A young bird is helpless without its mother who feeds it, teaches it to survive and protects it. As the chick's wings grow, like its mother it can soar and reach far distances, having outgrown its incapacity of youth. Someone who has been mentored or supported in a certain way but suddenly feels they are now bigger, better, or higher than their parent or mentor is said to have grown wings or "mile izimpiko."

For example, a child that grows up in a home where they dress a certain way or eat certain foods, grows up and leaves. When they return, they are disrespectful, argumentative and show disdain for the very lifestyle that nurtured them in their youth, unlike before they had "grown wings."

Too big for his britches

85

Induka enhle igawalwa ezizweni

The good stick is cut from distant lands

Some of the best things come from afar

Zulu people like foreign things when they bring value. The most prized stick is the one procured from a distant place. In marriage, the spouse that has come into the family from far away is often considered more interesting. They'll likely have a different upbringing and way of thinking that will enrich and improve the family.

86

Yazwela elimele

The one that is hurt moos first

Those who are wounded make the most noise

Raising cattle requires farmers to have grazing grounds, breeding pens, hygiene regimens and health standards. Maintaining the latter most often involves treating the entire herd with medicine. For the cows and bulls that are healthy, the medicine is preventative care. However, for the cattle that are hurt or sick, the medicine is a slightly painful treatment. Farmers can easily spot which cow is hurt by how they react to the medicine. Those that are hurt are the first to moo as the medicine enters their wounds and cuts.

Like cattle, people can be easily identified as someone who is hurt or wounded by an issue when they quickly speak up about a general statement. For example, a man says, "Marriage is a beautiful institution," and two people quickly speak up about how marriage is awful. One may assume that those people have been hurt by marriage and the emotional wound has not healed because they were the first to "moo."

DISCRETION

87

Ukudonsa umuntu ngedlebe

To pull (a person) by the ear

Caution, warn, painstakingly advise

A tug of the earlobes, a stern look, a quiet tone, close proximity and annunciated speech lets every child know their parent is saying something serious and something important. The saying 'ukudonsa ngedlebe' figuratively embodies these actions to mean earnestly and sincerely giving someone advice or warning.

Take someone to the side

88

Indlebe iyaphinga

The ear is promiscuous

The ear hears everything

In public you hear many sounds and talk without distinction. You may inadvertently hear a beautiful song, a sweet conversation or even a terrible argument you would rather not have. Unfortunately, we do not have the ability to strain what goes to our ears. Our ears do not need permission in order to hear something, and they hear it all! This colorful expression is not considered impolite.

The walls have ears

89

Ithi ingaba nkulu ingazekeki

Once a story becomes big, it is hard to recount

What a story!

When Zulu speakers are dealing with a serious matter, one which they need to tell someone and proceed to sort out, they will often preface their account by saying, ironically, 'ithi ingaba nkulu ingazekeki' ('Once a story [or matter] becomes big [or serious], it is hard to recount'). This is to mean that what they are dealing with is just bewildering, upsetting, ridiculous, or shocking. This is often used also by the person being told about a serious matter, one that is hard to believe.

What a doozy!

90

Ukukhahlelwa ihhashi esifubeni

To get kicked by a horse on the chest

To tattle

When someone cannot keep a secret, Zulu speakers will tell them, "wakhahlelwa ihhasi esifubeni (you were kicked by a horse on the chest)." This expression compares the actions of a person that cannot keep things to themselves, to the effects of being kicked in the chest by a horse. Meaning, your chest/heart, where secrets should be kept, is cracked open and, therefore unable to keep anything hidden. Additionally, horses are known for neighing whenever it sees or feels anything amiss. The horse is an apt symbol of a person who cannot keep anything to themselves and divulges or 'neighs' everything out at the slightest provocation.

To let the cat out of the bag
Someone who can't hold water

91

Ukukubeka kucace okwezinqe zesele

To make it as clear as a frog's buttocks

To make it abundantly clear

Zulu culture encourages a healthy relationship with the human body. In turn, Zulu people, generally, have quite a positive image and are not shy about discussing body parts; so much that they have even included them in their sayings and expressions. This saying is one of those and it is not considered impolite at all. When someone is clear and precise in their speech, leaving no room for ambiguity or misinterpretation, Zulu speakers will often say 'ukubeke kwacaca okwezinqe zesele (you put it as clear as a frog's buttocks)'. In the same manner, a frog is unclothed and has its backside out for all to see at all times; a precise person's speech is clear to everyone listening.

To make it crystal clear

92

Ukudla indlebe

To eat each other's ears

Discreetly talk to or alert someone

When people are having a discreet conversation in front of others, each person will usually whisper in the other's ear while standing close to them. They are so close that it looks like they are eating or biting each other's ears. Well, according to Zulu speakers, anyway. This common expression is used any time a people tell each other something that is not known to many others, whether they do so in public or not. It is also used when they warn one another of something. So when people are involved in such a conversation, Zulu speakers will say 'badlana indlebe' ('they are eating each other's ear'). If it's a one-way disclosure or warning, in other words, only one person is doing the talking or warning, the '-ana' reciprocal suffix is removed, and it is 'udla indlebe' (he/she is eating the ear'). Sometimes Zulu speakers may use the verb 'luma' ('bite') instead of 'dla' ('eat') with this expression.

To have a tête-à-tête.
To give a heads up

93

Ukukhuluma uze wome amathe

To talk until one's saliva dries

To talk a lot

Whenever a person talks frequently to another, especially to caution or advise them about something, Zulu speakers will say 'ukhulume waze woma amathe' ('he/she spoke until his/her saliva dried out'). In other words, the person addressed a topic extensively, to the point of exhaustion. Your mother telling you to stop doing something that you continue doing or a teacher warning you about the importance of studying for the final when you still do not are examples of situations in which they would use this expression. The people have been speaking and cautioning continually until they ran out of 'saliva.' Additionally, while it is possible to literally talk until your mouth is dry, this saying is also used as a hyperbole to mean that someone has run out of energy.

To wax lyrical
To talk until you are blue in the face

94

Ukugeqa amagula

To tip the gourds

To tell everything

In a traditional Zulu home, igula or a calabash is very important as a form of Tupperware. The fruit's gourd is dried out and typically used to store milk and mature it into *amasi* or sour cream, which Zulu people love. When the people did eventually enjoy the sour cream, we can imagine they were sparing, knowing the long process it took to produce it. So, when someone shares information fully and completely with others, be it through a story, speech, lecture, or confession, Zulu speakers liken this to someone emptying the calabashes of all their contents such that there is nothing else to consume. It is telling that the expression uses the plural 'amagula,' meaning this is about emptying not just one but numerous calabashes of their contents. A tell-all interview with Oprah by a public personality, where they divulge all the juicy details of their life, is an example of *ukugeqa amagula*.

Spill the beans

95

Ukuchathazela

To pour a little bit for someone

Tell a little or give a tip-off

There are times that you may not want to tell someone everything, but just want to divulge enough to get them off your back or warn them. Wanting to give only minimum information is compared to someone who has a drink and wants to share only a little bit with someone. It is important to note that Zulu speakers could have used the verb 'thela (pour)' for this expression but used 'chathaza (pour in a small quantity)' instead, which is accurate in conveying the exact sentiment. So when someone tells you something in small details, Zulu speaker will say 'uyakuchathazela (they are pouring a little bit for you)'. The expression is also used when someone tells you something you are not supposed to or expected to know, like tipping off authorities about a crime.

To let something slip

96

Ukukhala kwesisicathulo

The stomping of the shoe

To have final authority

This expression is used when identifying a person who is in charge in any setting. Whether it is a boss at work, a parent, or a captain of a ship, if they have the ultimate word on things, Zulu speakers will often say "Kukhala esakhe isicathulo (It is his/her shoe that stomps)." The origins of this expression certainly belong to the colonial era as it involves shoes. Most official colonial buildings, like hospitals or police stations, had wooden floors. People's footsteps were quite audible. People likely observed that authority figures in these places routinely stomped one or both feet on the ground, making a sound with their shoes. Whether it was a supervisor signaling their sudden presence to absent-minded staff or indicating an end of a meeting, this practice became synonymous with stomping one's authority.

To be the top dog
To be the 'captain'
To have the say-so

GROWING UP

97

Ubudoda abukhulelwa

Manhood need not be grown up to

Age is not the marker of manhood or womanhood.

Maturity is not reached through simply growing older. It is attained by consistently making wise choices in all types of circumstances.
Working consistently, maintaining a marriage, taking care of children and respecting elders are just a few ways someone can demonstrate maturity. Someone who does these is no longer a child, but a man/woman, even if they are young. On the other hand, someone who struggles to exhibit such maturity may not be considered to have entered man/womanhood, no matter their age.

Age is just a number

98

Umthente uhlaba usamila

A plant/tree is sharper when it has just come out of the ground

Seeing the good one while it's young

Think of the classic story of an older mentor and his young, zealous, energetic and optimistic mentee. Throughout the storyline, the mentor maintains their relationship because he sees an unrefined talent within the mentee that could be trained and honed for greatness.

Zulu people generally embrace the process of aging because they embrace and celebrate all stages of life.

Youth is attributed with beauty, strength and sharpness/mental agility. Recognizing and cultivating these attributes forms the foundation of mentoring, an important part of Zulu culture and history.

99

Akukho sihlala saguga namagxolo aso

There is no tree that gets old with its (fruits/leaves)

The things that made you great....you don't take them to old age

The Zulu people are not afraid of getting old. They embrace the process of aging and not only the wisdom and respect associated with getting older but also the changes to the body and mind. Just like a tree doesn't grow old with its fruits, people usually don't continue to produce with the same vigor and force they did in their youth. The fastest runners become slow, the greatest thinkers begin to forget, and even the strongest people become weak. It is accepted as a good and natural part of life and not anything of which someone should be ashamed or apprehensive.

www.ingramcontent.com/pod-product-compliance
Lightning Source LLC
Chambersburg PA
CBHW021114080526
44587CB00010B/514